I Remember

All of the parts of the body holds memories in a very unique
way
Memories that got me to where I am today
What memories does it hold might you ask
The memories of the fling that we're in

My heart and eyes holds all of the times whenever you came
into my sight
My mouth and laughter holds all of the times you made me
laugh and all of the "I love yous"
My hands holds all of the times that I held yours
My arms holds all of the times where you needed a hug
My lips and neck holds all of the times you gave me the
most deepest of satisfaction
My shoulders holds all of the times where you just needed
someone to lean on
My brain holds all of the times where you were the only one
I was thinking about
My smile holds all of the times where you have brightened
up my day
My legs and feet holds all of the times where we have
danced under the midnight moon
My ears holds all of the times where you have whispered all
of those sweet words
See what I mean when I say my body holds all of those
memories
I love what you have gave me and would do it all again if I
could

A Trusting Love

I was told never to trust a smiling face
But it wasn't until after the fact that it was my life that you
chose to grace
It was my time that you chose to waste
You gave me the heartbreak of the worst case
You made me the happiest person in the world
But I don't know if I can say I made you feel the same way
I tried loving you better than the last girl did
But you broke my heart before I can even begin
Was the love I gave you not enough
If you would've given me a chance I could've given you the
love you deserve
They say not to trust someone with a smiling face
I guess you can say that I learned it a little too late

Ebony and Ivory #88

I am a piano player figuring out my next best song. I sit in front of those keys hoping for something to come out of my heart and soul. The longer I sit here, the more pain I try to conjure up. As time moved on, I thought of the greatest pain that I ever thought of: the day you chose to walk out of my arms and life and into hers. The day you told me that you fell out of love with me and that you fell in love with her was one of the worst days of my life. From that day on to that moment on the piano, I chose to not let my mouth do all of the talking. Instead, I chose to let my heart, soul, tears, pain, and fingers do all of the talking. I let all of those things out as I started to play. The more music I played, the more of a story I was starting to write. By the time I finished playing, the pain went away. This is the story of how I turned my pain into music.

Sonnet of Love

My love for you is all unrequited
Something I would not mind waiting for me
This love I have is now all admitted
I am the right one just you wait and see

All my love for you is nothing but sweet
It is nothing short of a lovely dream
It won't be long until our two hearts meet
We're nothing but two fish swimming upstream

I wish to love you with all of my might
Being with you would be out of this world
Me loving you would be too out of sight
The one wish I have is to be your girl

I hope this dream of mine will come true
I wish I can share this sweet dream with you

Just Why

When Mary J. Blige said "I can't get enough of you"
I felt every bit of it as my mind goes right to you
I can't get enough of the fact that your smile is one thing that
keeps me going
How I wish to taste the sweetness that you call lips
How I wonder if they're as sweet as honeycombs or as sweet
as brown sugar
How good I feel every time you look in my direction
Everytime you bite your lips makes my knees weak and my
heartbeat quicken
How I get butterflies in my stomach every time you creep
into my mind
You are the reason why I act like a schoolgirl with a crush
around you
Every chance I get, I would think how sweet my first name
sound next to your last name
I blame no one else but you for making me feel the way I do
When Mary J. Blige said "I can't get enough of you"
Damn, she wasn't lying

Love and Hate

There's a thin line between love and hate
Sometimes the 2 are blurred together
How often I ask myself why do I both hate and love you
Like how I love and hate the way you look at me across the
room
How every time we do so much as touch, it's like speaking a
language only we know
How I both love and hate how I can't get through a day
without you whispering my name in my ear
How every time you pull away I always manage to pull you
back in
I just can't handle the fact that I love it when you come
But hate it when you leave
There's a thin line between love and hate
Sometimes the 2 are blurred together
How I managed to both love and hate you
I guess I will never know the answer

School Love

I'm walking down the school hallways to my next class as if any student would

I see the girls adjusting their lip gloss and the boys slapping palms

If this day could get any more normal, I see a face that I am way too familiar with

A face that made everything and everyone just not exist anymore

It was as if the whole universe was just created for me and him

My face would sting with embarrassment and fluster the moment he looked at me

Everytime he smiled, I have never failed to get weak at the sight of that smile

My heart would beat a million times a minute when he talked to me

But my tongue would be tied to the max everytime I tried to talk to him

I have always visualized us walking down the halls holding hands and starting a romance with each other

I get butterflies at the thought of my first name right next to his last name

Everything goes back to normal and he walks past me

Giving me the feeling of heaven once again

Can this honestly be all a dream

Because if it is, please don't wake me up

Kickball of Love

Remember as kids we used to play catch
How nothing but our innocence and giggles seem to fill the
air
How we manage to catch the other's throw
Years later, we still managed to play catch
But this time, not with a red rubber kickball
This time around, we traded in our kickball for our hearts
This time, innocence is being blown away and romance is
filling it in
How could I not see that my childhood friend would be the
person I fell in love with
How could I not feel the attraction in the beginning
How can I tell you without my heart getting broken in the
mix
Before I reveal this secret to you, I have a question
Would you catch my heart and I catch yours like we did
back in childhood
Or would you let mine crush to the ground

Dancing After Dark

I am in a sleazy, empty nightclub in a rough neighborhood. Neon lights flicker in and out as graffiti covers most of the walls both inside and out. The scent of alcohol and broken hearts seems to linger on through the air of the night. I sit at the bar and take in the intro of "Careless Whisper" by George Michael. To my right, I see a stranger in black. His black dress shoes, pants, and Polo shirt compliments his sweet chocolate skin. His dark eyes gave me the message that I have met him somewhere before. As the song goes on, he leads me to the middle of the empty dance floor. Instead of words, we held a conversation through our dance moves. His dancing and the way he touched my body gave me a sensual and provocative feeling. Did we meet somewhere else in the past? Another time? By the time the song was over, there was no one else in sight. Was everything in my head?

Savory

Intoxication ain't even the word to describe our chemistry
Or even the times we have spent in your car
Every time we have kissed, you never failed to take me to
new heights
The more intimate things have gotten
The higher you have managed to take me
The level of satisfaction you gave me is through the roof
The more time we have spent together
The higher the chance of that chemistry never leaving
Every time you kissed my neck
My soul never fails to leave my body
Is this what heaven is supposed to feel like
If so, then I will never want to leave this place

Heart of Memories

My heart is like a memory book
Full but yet somehow invisible
My heart was the place that the memories of me and you
took place
Each of which made me fall in love with you even more
You never failed to give me the light in my eyes
Every memory I thought I was going to cherish for life
But it turns out that I was extremely wrong and blindsided
All of a sudden, you started to back away from me
The more you stayed away from me
The less memories we made together and you made
memories with someone else
You took away the light in my eyes and gave it to someone
else
For my eyes are filled with tears
I have looked at you like a saint
But how I was wrong
We were once close lovers
But now we have become 2 strangers with memories

Young Infatuation

I remember seeing you coming down the hall before first
period
Running faster than the speed of light to make it just before
the bell rings
Just me seeing you first thing in the morning and the last
thing in the afternoon was the highlight of my day
And the way the morning sun was hitting your sweet,
chocolate face at the perfect angle
Every time I saw you, a knot of excitement never failed to
show up in my stomach
How I always fantasized running into your arms and you
catching me
Telling each other that we don't want to let the other go
Just hearing your laughter as you run just makes my heart
skip a beat
And that it plays a never-ending melody in my mind
How in the world did God make someone like you just so
perfect
How did he know that you needed to be placed in my life
How I wish that I knew the answers to those questions
But I guess that I will never know those answers

Soul Stirring

Heartbreak is the emotion that stirs my soul
A well-known guest that never seems to leave
And one that somehow knows my name
How I find myself to be heartbreak's most known victim
How I manage to get my foot in the door of love
But somehow heartbreak snatches by my shirt collar and
drags me
How can something be so normal but yet so brutal and ugly
No matter how much I try to hide from it
Heartbreak never fails to creep up on me when I least expect
it to

Traumatic Love

I held his hand daydreaming of what what we would become
How we would become both lovers and friends rolled up
into one
Or how Daniel Caesar had said it
"How I will be the Tylenol he takes when his head hurts"
And how he'll be the Tylenol for my headaches
How he will be the one thing that's on my mind day in and
day out
Just like how I'm on his mind 24/7
But this love isn't what it's cracked up to be
He let the trauma of his past love get the best of him
And somehow let his trauma out on me
I was strong enough to end it as it torn me
His trauma took a toll on me
I held his heart while having nightmares of what I just ended
Now that I'm in a different place in my life
I now am taking a journey to individual freedom

Current Lover

Things you said after I met your current lover
How she was the best thing that ever happened to you
How she always managed to make your gray skies blue
Or how she manages to be the sun of your universe
Did it ever run through your mind that I wish to be in her
shoes
You are the main person I think about day in and day out
Not only you were the sun of my universe
You were my whole universe wrapped up in one person
I wished that you will be the best thing to ever happen to me
But somehow you saw me as the friend who was always
there for you
The friend you come to when times were rough
I will remain the friend who was dedicated to you from the
start
Though I was too late to say anything to you
Just know that I'm happy for you

A Sweet Touch

If I had to describe your touch, it'd be so sweet it could be
nearly forbidden
Just you in my sight sends me to another dimension
You satisfy my body in a way no one else can
We've both seen a side of each other that was both soft and
vulnerable
The more we spend away from each other
The more of you I end up craving
I never knew that there was a touch as sweet as yours
Just by looking in those sexy brown eyes made me realize
that possibilities were more than endless
You gave me the satisfaction I never knew I needed
You explored my body in a way that thrilled me
I never want this thrill to end

Falling Hard

Out of the 7 billion plus people in this world
You're the one I feel heavily for
The one who I just can't stop crushing on
The one who I imagined a whole future together
From dancing to our first song as husband and wife
To watching our future children grow up
You're the one who I just can't stop thinking about day in
and day out
How the excitement never fails to come when you come to
mind
How for some reason I can feel your presence near me
Even though you're not around, how at night I can feel the
spirit of your hand caress my body ever so gently
It's funny how you're the only person who ever made me
feel this way
I wish that you can understand that what I'm feeling for you
is real
But at the end of the day, you told me that you weren't ready
for a relationship with me yet
And trust me, I understand
But just remember that you'll always be the one who I feel
heavily for

To the Girls Who Came Before Me

To the girls who came before me and broke his heart and
spirit
I hope that you guys are happy
You had a rare treasure and didn't know what to do with it
You treated him the same way your old beau treated you
Like trash
You broke his heart before he had the chance to show you
what real love is
Because you were scared he was going to be like the rest
So he came to me with his broken heart and his guard up
high
As well as emotional trauma and trust issues
His past of bad love will end right here and right now
I want him to know that true love is beautiful
And not every woman's intentions on loving him are untrue
That the true love that he was dreaming of for years actually
exists
How his wants and needs only needed to be expresses once
and not to be forgotten
So to all of the girls who came before me and broke his heart
and spirit
I hope that you're really happy now
I wish that I can say that violence is the answer for each and
every last one of you
All I want to say is thank you
Thank you for letting me have the chance to treat the way
you should've done a long time ago

Begging for Love

I begged for your love when I know I shouldn't have
Though I gave you all of mine
I gave you all of the time and effort in the world
When I couldn't even get a slither of yours
As scared as I am of losing you
Are you even scared of losing me at all
Did it ever cross your mind at all
Just like how it has crossed mine
Love shouldn't have to be begged for
But why am I begging for yours when I give you all of mine
While loving you, I somehow managed to lose myself
Now that we are no longer together
I'm now on the search of finding myself

A New Love's Promise

I met you when you were picking up the pieces of your
broken heart
How you were trying to heal from the last girl you were with
Before this love thing has started between us, you were
scared to give someone your love
For it wasn't valued for what it was worth to begin with
She forced you to pay the price of her romantic mistakes
And caused you to guard your heart with all of your might
How can I make you see that love isn't always a losing game
That you will no longer be the victim of someone else's
mistakes
That love's number one symptom isn't always known to be
pain
I promise to not let my past get the best of me and make me
hurt you
I promise that I'd not only show you love
I will show you things like bliss, splendor and intense
rapture
I must admit that love may be scary
But I promise you I will bring you to the light

My Love

My love for you is like a child and his teddy bear
Nothing but sweetness and innocence
A love that's never-ending like the nighttime sky
Nothing but the sole light of the moon and stars giving the
sky light kisses
My love for you is like a burning desire
Nothing but passion and a fiery inferno
My love for you is so beautiful that Romeo and Juliet can't
seem to compare
But there's something that I can't seem to get out of my
head
While my pure intentions are nothing but to love and cherish
you for all time
Why are you so busy loving someone else who's love is not
even half of the love that I got?

Time Never Slows (For Me and You)

You are the cause of my fast beating heart
The way my knees quake whenever I hear your voice
How I try to savor every moment that we have together
But time never seems to stop for me when our time together
is over
How is it that you're my favorite hello but my hardest
goodbye
You know as much as I love talking on the phone with you
It never beats seeing you in person
How not only I can hear your angelic yet husky voice
I can be able to feel you physically
I can feel the way your arms wrap around me
How I wish I can hold you for all eternity, but knowing that
I can't
Ain't it funny how this love thing works
It's something me and you will laugh at for hours

Love is (The Greatest Fear)

I am rummaging through my mementos from my time of
love lane
I noticed something that's split into two
It's a picture of me and you from our time together torn in
half
When I see this picture, tears suddenly flood my eyes
The intensity of your gaze from that picture makes my
stomach do a flip
The memories of you and I start to hit me like a tidal wave
The times you made me smile gave me nostalgic
The times you made me cry gave me great pain
Like the complete tear of this picture, you never failed to
tear each of my heartstrings one by one
The day that we met and the day I was able to call you mine,
you told me that we were going to be together forever and
you'll always be by my side
Where were you when I needed you the most?
Now that I am looking at this picture, it resembles nothing
but my heart: broken and tattered

Torn Memories

I am rummaging through my mementos from my time of
love lane
I noticed something that's split into two
It's a picture of me and you from our time together torn in
half
When I see this picture, tears suddenly flood my eyes
The intensity of your gaze from that picture makes my
stomach do a flip
The memories of you and I start to hit me like a tidal wave
The times you made me smile gave me nostalgic
The times you made me cry gave me great pain
Like the complete tear of this picture, you never failed to
tear each of my heartstrings one by one
The day that we met and the day I was able to call you mine,
you told me that we were going to be together forever and
you'll always be by my side
Where were you when I needed you the most?
Now that I am looking at this picture, it resembles nothing
but my heart: broken and tattered

Melodic Love

My heart is nothing but an old piano
Something that's getting older and older with time
My love is like a sweet melody
Something that's unwritten and incomplete
My soul is like a theater
Something nothing other than empty
One after the 0ther, my past lovers couldn't play the melody
of my heart
When you came along, you played something different
Something that was light and beautiful
For once you have played my melody right
Thanks to you, my heart feels young again
Thanks to you, my melody feels written and complete
Thanks to you, my soul's theater has filled, giving us a
standing ovation

The Power of Love

I live in a world where the gods and the goddesses come
together as one
From Artemis all the way to Zeus, this world seems to be as
powerful as heaven itself
As I walk through this world of power, I come to find
someone with no familiarity whatsoever
I come to see the features of his face as they were strong but
gentle and sweet as well
I saw the burning sweetness of his eyes and the crisp cold of
the smile on his face
The mystery of his being has grabbed me to the core
The more he stared at me, the more that my heart started to
skip a massive beat
He rose before me and came more and more close to where
we almost touch each other
His slightly warm breath started giving me the most purest
of pleasure
Butterflies started forming inside of me when he started to
pull me into him
We were like fire and ash
So similar but yet so different at the same time
He was beautiful and lively
With a little bit of destructive
And I was lost and scared
And also totally in love with him

When our lips touched, the power of the earth surrounded us with its presence
If love making is something like this, then I wouldn't want it to be any other way
I live in a world where the gods and the goddesses come together as one
Who knew that this world feels as powerful as I feel kissing this god right now

Late Night Confessional

You make my heart skip a beat
Just me hearing your voice is nothing more than sweet
I wonder if I told you I love you, would you ever say it back
Just know that I do and that's for sure a fact
I have always fantasized you whispering in my ear
Saying that it's me you'll always be near
Every love song that I hear on the radio is the words I wish
to say to you
Only me and my heart knows that it's true
Every love poem I wrote I only have you as my own
protagonist
I'm just simply in love you can't you get the gist
Every night you are in my dreams
You're the only one that I dream of so it seems
You holding me close to your chest as I listen to the beat of
your heart
I hope that in life we will never part
What better feeling for me to feel than love
My one true confession is for me to spend all eternity with
you up above
As I finish off this confessional, know that everything I say
is true
Now I must bid you adieu

Monstrous

They say that you can't fall in love with a monster. I fell in love with one and he wasn't as monstrous as he seems to me. His eyes are windows no one even bothered to even look in. Inside, all of his demons have tried to his well-being in the core. He has tears in his eyes that have yet to be cried, for he cries himself to sleep every single night as the world continuously has turned his back on him. From head to toe, he's covered in battle scars from constantly having to fight by himself with his demons. He gets himself lost in the music that he listens to so he can fill up the empty void that's on his body. His knuckles are bruised after he had to fight his way through society in order to find his acceptance from it. The pain was obviously visible all over his body and his mental state of mind. Since when was falling in love with monsters ever such a bad thing? The world told me that you can't fall in love with a monster. Who cares about what they say? I fell in love with one who isn't as monstrous as he seems to be to me

Love in Winter Wonderland

I am walking through an enchanted forest on a frosty winter night. The snow falling ever so angelically is cold to the touch as it hits my tongue while the cold December wind brushes up against me. The trees that are bare of their leaves are the homes of the small animals. As I continue making my way down this wintery path, I see an extremely faint silhouette that my mind just can't seem to make out in the slightest bit. As I begin to make my way towards this unfamiliar stature, it starts to become more and more clear with every single step. The unfamiliar stature turns out to be a man. He had lovely brown eyes that were mysterious, but yet sweet and gentle at the same time as his ebony skin is received by the light of the sole moon. His dark hair moves with the wind as blood rushes to his cheeks. His sweet lips slighted cold as he stood tall looking down at me. He held out his hand to me with a voice of sultry that sent butterflies to my stomach.

"May I have the pleasure of walking you through this dark forest?"

My heart skips a beat as I nod and put my hand into his. We walk through the forest as he whispers sweet sayings in my ear. By the end of our walk, he gives me a beautiful flower and we share a kiss that not only warms up our bodies, but our souls.

Old Jazz Love

I am sitting alone in an old jazz nightclub. The air is so seemingly filled with jazz, heartbreak, one night stands and regrets. As I sit alone, I hear a voice that's filled with heavy melodic pain. I turn my attention to a swooning male jazz singer grace the stage. His voice and deep brown eyes are filled with pain as if he was hurt one too many times. He has dreamy black hair oh so neatly done. His rich ebony skin glistened under the stage lights. He stands majestically on stage singing of love, leaving the room and my body unbelievably intoxicated. He walks to my seat and serenades me with his sultry voice as he takes my hand raising it to his lips kissing it ever so softly. When the song was over, he placed his lips on mine, causing the room to vanish completely. Oh what a night.

My Secret Lover

I have a secret to tell you. I wish I can tell you but until then this is the closest way for me to say it. I like you. There are a million things that I like about you. I love the way your eyes light up everytime you talk about your passions. I love the way you are able to make me smile, even when I'm upset. I love the way you make me laugh. And that smile. That smile. That smile is one of the most charismatic smiles I have ever seen in my life. It's strange to see anyone resist a smile like the one you have. I wish you can see that I can treat you better than the last one can. Now that my secret's out, may I ask you will you put my heart in your hands and carry it like I am willing to do with you.

A Game Called Love

Love can be defined in more than a million ways. To me, love is like a game. It has nothing but 2 outcomes: you can either win at love or lose at love. In life, love is one of the most dangerous games that's ever to be played. No one tells you the rules of love. You figure them all out as you go through life. If I ever had the chance to tell someone who isn't following the rules of love, the first thing I would say is, "You are playing a dangerous game without so much as a glimpse into the rule book"

I Once Knew A Love

I once knew a love that was sweet
A love that gave me the strength to believe in love one more
time
Even when I couldn't find the strength to believe in it myself
It was the love that made me believe in it myself
It was the love that made me believe that love can conquer
all
This love was the purest of pure
This love was so pure it had smoldered within my heart for
all eternity
This love was too beautiful to look at
Now that this love is a once-was, you caused me to believe
that I'm not worthy of love
But just know it's not over for me yet

The Land of 2 Lovers

When we met, we knew nothing of each other. We were 2 different people with 2 totally different personalities. As time went on, we started becoming like 2 peas in a pod. You told me about all of the demons that you were dealing with and fighting as I was able to tell you about mine. We often stayed up until 4AM having nothing but sacred conversations with one another. Me and you started falling in love with each other at the drop of a coin. Everything changed when she suddenly came into the picture. No questions asked, you suddenly were in her arms instead of mine. Instead of being your most prized possession in your eyes, I turned into a toy being sat on the shelf to be played with whenever you were ready to play with me. I thought you were going to help me make my demons go away, not make more and make things worse for me. Now that you 2 are together, I am nothing but an emotionless body with so much to say to you, 3 particular questions that I really want to ask you: What does she have that I don't, was I ever even worthy of your love, and where was the boy that I soon started falling in love with at the beginning.

Things I Wish I Can Say To You

Things I wish to say to you
One: you take place in my dreams
Can you take place in my reality
I dream of you in my dreams every night
The way you look at me is beyond compare
Two: if your love was a pill, I'd take it everyday without
hesitation
Your kisses are like drugs
No matter how sweet they are, they are extremely addicting
Sending me to rehab for repeatedly wanting to taste your lips
is an understatement
Three: you are the music to my ears
Whenever I hear your voice, my heart beats on the down
beat.
Every love song doesn't compare to my feelings for you
I will never say these things that I want to say to you
I definitely know the damage that it would do and cause
I love you more than I hate my loneliness and pain

Dear Heartbreak

Dear Heartbreak

Hello darling. We are long overdue for a chat. Like your twin, love, you are a very old friend of mine. As much as I want to say that I despise you with a burning passion, there's a part of me that I can't. You forced me to keep my guard down when it came to those who walked into my life. You made me the most vulnerable at the wrong time with the wrong people. You made me experience the sort of pain that I would've never dreamed of experiencing. Though you caused me nothing but trauma throughout my life, all I want to say is thank you. Thank you for teaching me to not let my guard down for everyone. Thank you for teaching me to be vulnerable with the right people. Lastly, thank you for teaching me that I'm going to experience the worst type of pain in order to see the end of the rainbow. Thank you for making me a really strong person.

Sincerely

Sydney

Euphoria (The Feeling of Passion)

I am sitting in my room with a book in my hands. The cover is light green with darker green speckled dots carelessly scattered across the front and back. Across the front has the following word spelled out: "Diary". As I hold this beautiful, prized possession in my hands, I flip through page after page. Each page represents a time of my past, from every bittersweet kiss that I have ever had to every single heartbreak that I have ever experienced. After moments of flipping through my past, I stumble across a page that sends me into nothing but arousal. A page that I never spoke about to a single soul. That steamy page was about me making love to you. It brought me the same feelings now as it did the day I wrote it. Like now, you were the only person that was ever on my mind. I just wished to feel your lips press gently and slowly down my neck, back, shoulders, and chest. Just the thought of you kissing all over my body gives me goosebumps to the core and makes my heart beat rapidly. Have I ever told you that you were the reason why I never succeeded to fully control myself. The more I think about you and your kiss, the more euphoria I tend to feel. Before I close my diary, I have one more thing to say to you: I can honestly say that I love the way that you make me feel inside and out.

Battlescars

Me and my beloved are completely covered in scars. Though they are in different parts of our bodies, all of them tell the same exact story. You might ask us what story had given us all of those scars. All of those scars represent our love story and how we got to where we are today: through hell and hard times. At the end of the day, we were both able to get through the terrible times. We have been through and walked through hell so many times. I thank him for sticking by my side and staying with me in the worst of times. All of the stories in the world that was ever written, our love story was the best that was ever written. Why would we hide our scars when they all tell the world such a beautiful love story?

The Last Wish

They say "Sewing a nightmare was quick and easy and dreams take months and cost a fortune". These vivid motion pictures that I had were simply anything close to nightmares. They were all blissful dreams with the one person that I have favored the most: you, the way your hand cupped my small round face sent me butterflies in my stomach. The way my body followed the rhythm of your matched the syncopation of the flames of desire in my heart. The way your sweet, baritone voice constantly says my name in my ear has lifted me. They say "Sewing a nightmare was quick and easy and dreams take months and cost a fortune". These vivid motion pictures that I had were simply anything close to nightmares. They were all blissful dreams with the one person that I have favored the most: you, the way your hand cupped my small round face sent me butterflies in my stomach. The way my body followed the rhythm of your matched the syncopation of the flames of desire in my heart. The way your sweet, baritone voice constantly saying my name in my ear has lifted me up to the heavens making me not want to come back down to planet earth again. Nothing is more delightful than dreaming of you giving me the purest of pleasure that's out of this world. Can I ask you something? Will you ever bother in making my dream into a reality? You taking me up to the heavens is making me not want to come back down to planet earth again. Nothing is more delightful than dreaming of you giving me the purest of pleasure that's out of this world. Can I ask you something? Will you ever bother in making my dream into a reality?

Dancing After Dark: The Morning After

The morning after, I wake up in the comfort of my home with a slight hangover. I try to recollect what happened with the handsome stranger that I met and danced with the night before. Was it a dream like I thought it was or was it just mere reality? As I get out of bed to get dressed and head out the door, I go to a cafe not too far from that same sleazy club I was at the night before. Sitting outside the cafe, I see a man that looks familiar to me, reading a newspaper and drinking a cappuccino. The closer I got to the cafe, I couldn't believe my eyes. It was the same man that I danced with the night before. This time he was wearing something similar from the night before. He looks up from his newspaper with the same dark eyes that greeted me the night before. The sultriness and the sensuality were still there with just a bit of sweetness. My mind goes back to that provocative dance that we had shared the night before as "Careless Whisper" starts playing in my mind. He gets up and we tend to meet in the middle. He pulls me in by my waist as if he was saying "It's you again" and kisses me with such a deep passion. His full lips being soft and sweet. I guess it was mere reality after all.

I Want The The of Love

I crave the type of love where we can finish each other's sentences
As well as one of us, weirdly say what the other one was thinking
I crave the type of love that even after we pursued each other initially
We're still finding ways to capture each other's love and heart
I crave the type of love where we pray for each other
As well as with one another
I crave the type of love where stepping out isn't the solution every time we fight
I crave the type of love where we're not only satisfied by physical touch
But satisfied to be in each other's presence
I crave the type of love where we're not ashamed to show each other off
To let the whole world know that this is my person
I crave the type of love where we could just be ourselves
Without worrying about being judged by the other person
I crave the type of love that he lets me have my moments
And allows me to be vulnerable and I do the same thing with him
I crave the type of love where when we're not in each other's presence, we're thinking about each other
But until the day that special person comes with that love

I will be praying for them both

Both Sides of Love

I'm like Leon Bridges when he sings his song "Beyond"
I find it humorous how love can make us act
It can bring out the very best in us
While it can bring out the very worst in us as well
Love can bring out the positive pride in us
As it will bring out the very jealous side of us at times
I love the beauty of love that's being sung about
That it made me believe in soul mates once again as well as
love
As beautiful and ugly love can be seen or portrayed
Love can be also complicated and uneasy
Especially on the complicated part
I couldn't help but getting ahead of myself with this poem
For love is one of the most bittersweet things on the planet.

My Favorite Love Song

What if I told you you became the lyrics to my favorite love songs
How I smile like a fool everytime you cross my mind
Or just so happen to even see you in person
How can my heart not beat fast everytime I see you
I don't think that anyone has me geeked out the way that you do
In the sweetest way, you turned my whole world upside down
And I don't think that I want it to be right side up
How can the heavens craft someone so beautifully
From the crown of your head to the soles of your feet
Just you alone is just breathtakingly heavenly
I can't say that I have to admit it
But you're the reason why my favorite love songs exists

Love (Through His POV)

All of the angels up there in heaven and she's the only one
on this earth
How can God craft someone so beautiful with his extremely
heavenly hands
From those sexy brown eyes with hints of gold and honey of
hers that causes earthquakes
That lights up everytime I hear her talk about her passions
and dreams
To her smile that makes me gush everytime I see it
How every strand of her coily 4c black hair falls perfectly in
place
How her nose crinkles everytime I hear that beautiful
laughter of hers
As well as seeing those round, rosy cheeks raise up as well
And how her dark brown skin is so smooth and sweet
When I see her walk, it's like everything else completely
stops
Seeing her move her curvaceous hips with every step is like
a moment of fresh air
With each and every step, every man and woman takes a
double take to look at her
How her body, curvaceous and full, is so beautifully sweet
I can see the confidence that she portrays
Like Carl Carlton said, "She's poetry in motion"
She's her own definition of sexy and smart at the same time
Her calm and sweet demeanor takes my breath away
From head to toe, She's a work of art, oh so lovely
Out of all of the angels up there in heaven

God has spared this angel of beauty just for me

It's Me This Time

I never wanted to hurt him. I just wanted to go back and change things. I went and put my own selfish needs before his and I wish that I didn't. He did everything in his power to make me the happiest woman alive and I didn't even appreciate it one bit. He held my heart with caution while I broke his in a heartbeat. While he was busy loving me, I was too busy loving somebody else who clearly didn't give a damn about me. Now I'm the one who caused the tears he cried each and every night and I don't blame him one bit. If I can turn back the hands of time, I could've been a hell of a better woman to him. But I know that I can't do so. I know I have whatever is coming for me. He doesn't deserve a woman like me and deserves a woman that will love him a hell of a lot better than I can.

I Don't Want To Fall

I'm scared of falling, especially falling in love
Because I know if I was to fall in love, heartbreak would be
around the corner waiting for me
Instead of me falling in love, I just wish I can walk in love
Elegantly float in love as if I was walking on thin air
Or even dance my way into love
Just making my way to love where it's not so painful
As it would be if I was to fall in love with you
I don't want to bare to see the scrapes, bruises, and scratches
on my heart and soul
As well as the break in my heart if I was to fall in love with
the wrong person
Just to remind me of my route of falling in love with you
What can I say love can be a brutal battlefield
I just wish that it wasn't so brutal if I had to fall there

Let's Make It Count

Tomorrow isn't promised so let's make every second count
If the world was to end in 24 hours, there would be no one
else I would spend it
With other than you and you only
I would manage to savor each and every second I have
While doing all of the things that we love to do
Every second is precious so let's keep that in mind
So let's run away together and take it all in
Capture every scenic moment that we have
From watching the early morning sunrise
To watching the sunset ending our last day
To even witnessing the moon and stars coming into place in
the night sky
As night fall, all I ask you is to hold me real tight
Hold me like you never held me before
And I will do the same thing to you
After we make the most sweetest of love to each other
I'll advise you to simply not hold anything back
I want to savor you and your touch before it all disappears

Goodbye for Good

Love can be a powerful thing but can be real dangerous
when it's being gone about it wrong
What I'm trying to say is love can either make you or break
you
When it comes to love, not only my heart is involved,
My time and emotions are making their appearances as well
These 2 things are just as precious as my heart
If you end up fumbling with this trinity of mine
You might have made the biggest mistake of your life by
fumbling the best thing that ever happened to you
It's just the fact that you took for granted the main person
that was ten toes down for you
I saw a rare kind of potential in you that I didn't see in
anyone else
The kind that I thought you would've saw in me too
Though I'm not made of glass, my heart still breaks easily
Though outwardly I may walk away, inwardly the pain still
stays
I have all but one small request for you
When you see me grinding and with a new lover
Don't you dare ask me for a redo
Because at this point, you're not going to find someone like
me again
So sit down, take this L, and think about your actions
I have a feeling that you're going to be sitting there for a
while

Used to Be Hung Up on You

Back in the day, I was so hung up on you
Like Bruno said, "Cause my heart breaks when I hear your
name"
I just wasn't ready to grasp and accept the fact that we
weren't meant to be
Just even the thought of you being with another lover
Made me feel nothing but never-ending envy and rage
Thinking "What kind of love could she give you that I
couldn't?"
Like Mary said "I can love you better than she can"
When I tell you I hoped that the universe would bring us
together one way or another
That was the old lovestruck Sydney
Let me introduce you to the new and improved Sydney
I don't want anything to do with you romantically anymore
Honestly, those girls can really have you now
I'm actually good where I'm at right now
Like Leela said "You had a good thing, and you let it go"
And don't even try to get me back when I'm with another
man from my roster
I hope that you didn't think that was an option
If you do, I want you to do something for me
Why don't you do like Ray said and "Hit the road, Jack"
Unlike you, this man actually deserves me

The Best True Love

I find it extremely ironic that you're the only person I truly
loved
And the only person I still love to this day
But for some reason I can't bring myself to admitting it
Or even going as far as admitting it to you
I'm not sure if it's an insane amount of pride or ego
Or that I'm pretty sure I already know the answer to this
statement
That you're not ready to be in a relationship
Which by all means that I understand to the fullest extent
But there's something else that I need to admit to you
That I can't bring myself to love anybody else
The same exact way that I love you

Fear of Love

They say the only thing we have to fear is fear itself
How can this be any more true
When one of my biggest fears is me loving you
I know not to be afraid of my fear
And they aren't there to scare me
For they are there to let me know that something is worth
I'm scared to lose myself in the sake of loving you
Or that you might even love me for the same reason you did
before
How I'm sitting here contemplating loving you
If me being scared of loving you isn't silly, I don't know
what is
But I'll get over my fears one way or another
And then I can bring myself to loving you

Is It Worth A Try

I'm scared to love you
As much as I want to, I can't bring myself to do so
I'm afraid of what might happen if we gave this love thing another try
Will you show me that you have changed for the better
Or would your bad habits come back again like they did before
Will you be able to regain the trust in me that you have broken
Or will you continue to break it over and over again
Will you help me put back together the pieces of my broken heart
Or would you break it even smaller than it was before
Are you the new changed person that you mentioned to me multiple times before
Or is it just a cover-up that I have once known
You know if I just wasn't so scared, I would've loved you to death
I would've been able to trust you this time around
Or have my heart put back together again
And even see a brand new person in you standing before me
But when that day finally comes, that feeling of fear will always be inside of me
And it's up to you to show me with your actions

Satisfactory

How would you feel if I told you that you fill up the appetite
of my soul
Just by your presence, touch and your kiss
The longer that we aren't in each other's sight
The more I crave you and your heavenly bliss
The sweetness of you is just extremely indescribable
Chocolate ain't got nothing on you
As you constantly give me a sugar rush everytime I taste you
I just can't get enough of that sweet taste of your lips
How can something this sweet even be real and delectable
But I guess I'll never know the answer to my own question

Beyond the Soul

When one closes their eyes to sleep, they see darkness and skim dreams
When I close mine, I see something on the other side
Something that resembles the sweetness and beauty of heaven
Something that makes me excited to close my eyes over and over again
What is it that I am seeing
Easy, I can see you
I see your sweet lips drip with the sweetest of nectar
I see the way you stare at me as I stare at you
I see the way your deep brown eyes twinkle with every bit of the nighttime stars
I see how you smile with the sun beaming through
When one closes their eyes to sleep, they see darkness and skim dreams
When I close mine, I see you

Crossfire

Your betrayal to me was like a crossfire
Something that was totally unexpected
You told me that you loved me
As naive as I was, I fell for it and said I love you too
The more we said it, the more you came out unburned
The more we said it, the more I was completely charred
I meant it every time you said it
Why couldn't you do the same thing for me
Why was I the one destroyed and you weren't
I wish I would've known if I managed to read between the
lines
I wish I had left when I had the chance

Hellos and Goodbyes

One beautiful morning I woke up refreshed
The sun flooding my room with its rays
I gotten out of my bed with some spring in my step
Once dressed and standing outside, I feel the sun hitting me
with full force
I don't know what gives me more joy
The fields of lavender or running through them into your
arms
As my face lights up every time I see you
How safe I feel when I'm finally in your arms
As if the world can't get to me
How can a whole day with you feels like a few minutes
The world goes back to what it was
Once at home and back in bed, I have come to terms with
something
You are my favorite hello and my hardest goodbye

If Only (You'd Stick Around)

You told me that we were forever
It was supposed to be me and you against the world
You said to me that you had my back
Just like I said to you that I had yours
But you lied
You lied to me endlessly
You never failed to act as if we were over
But the truth is, we never really began
The more you lied, the harder it was for me to believe you
I saw the potential of starting something wonderful with you
But sadly you didn't see the same vision
So you ran
You ran off before you even gave me the chance to love you
You ran off before I can show you that love is so much more
than you'd experienced
If you only stuck around a little while longer
You would've knew that my love was so much more

Through the Other Side

I am roaming around this endless world with the pieces of a broken heart inside of me. I suddenly stumble upon a glass shard. I picked it up and looked in it to see what was on the other side. I see a girl on the other side who's world has been shattered as her lover was in the arms of another. The further he went away, the smaller her world seemed to be. As heartbroken as she was, a piece of the other remained with them: her for all of the right reasons, him for all of the wrong reasons. As I looked closely at them, I suddenly realized something. The shard of glass is reflecting me and my lover. I have found the last piece of my broken heart.

Game Changer

It's not you. It's me
I was the one who let their insecurities get the best of them
I turned a blind eye to your flaws
Thanks to that, now you're gone
I tried changing you into my wildest desires
But didn't get to consider your feelings
I left you with nothing but a scorched heart and me an
enlarged ego
I fell into the arms of another who ruined me like I did you
Now that he's gone and you're with someone new, there are
no words to describe how sorry I am
I hope she treats you so much better than me
Maybe one day we can try this love thing once again

Meant to Be

The scent of smoke filled the air surrounding us
The fact that you're here with me is indescribable
I don't ever want to take this moment back
I don't know what's more intoxicating
The hickory of your cologne or your lingering kiss
Was this moment between us reay meant to be
Were you meant to be in my life
Were I meant to put in your life too
Whatever the reason may be, I'm happy that you're here
I'm glad that you were place here to complete life with me
together

Why Didn't We Last

With you, I thought our love was going to last forever
I managed to put your heart on lockdown
But what did you do with mine
You managed to break it before anything began
You managed to let your destroyed ego destroy mine
I felt it in my soul that this love wasn't ordinary
That this love was nothing but special
I gave you my all and then some
While you gave me less than the bare minimum
Now that we are no longer together
While you continue destroying your ego
Mine is on the road to recovery

The Beauty from Within

I loved you even when you didn't love yourself
When you wished that your brown eyes were the color of the
ocean
When you wished that your ebony black hair was a bright
blond
When you wanted to look like all of the black men in
Hollywood
Can't you see how much it hurts me that you hate what you
see in the mirror
Haven't you realize that I fell in love with you for you
Haven't you realize that God has created you in his image
I saw the beauty that you couldn't see and fell in love with
you
Why can't you see that for yourself
How about you listen to me once
Let me be the one to tell you that you're beautiful
Let me be the one to tell you that I love you
Let me be the one to tell you that God has created you how
he saw fit
Why can't you stop wishing to change yourself
Out of the 7 billion people on this planet
I have chosen you

Don't Come Back

You told me that I was the only one for you
The woman that you want to spend the rest of your life with
The last one you want to see before you go to sleep
And the first thing you see when you wake up
The woman who could put a smile on your face
And the one to wipe your tears away
The moment you left, a piece of me had left
You chose to find your love in someone else
You chose to find love in someone who could care less
All I could say is I'm irreplaceable

Loyalty vs. Lies

I gave you my heart, time and patience
You failed to do the same
You managed to give me nothing but tears, pain, heartbreak, and anger
You lied to me and kept forbidden truths from me
You played with my heart when I did the total opposite
Don't you know how many times I wanted to walk away
But I somehow managed to give you chance after chance to do better
You never really accomplished proving me right
So now due to your never ending stupidity
I'm leaving you for once and for all
No more of your hidden truths and secrets
No more breaking my heart
No more pain to cause me
I'm gone

Internal Emotions

I carry feelings for you inside of me that I have yet to feel
Feelings that have yet to do nothing but flourish inside of me
How can feelings like these become so extremely
indescribable
How can all the times you have winked at me make me feel
like a hopeless romantic
How is it that every time you manage to charm me, I
somehow choke on my words
How I can immediately feel the heat of my color changing
face
Whenever you seem to look at me, I get nothing but
butterflies in my stomach
Everytime I find myself looking at your lips, I never fail to
find myself wanting to kiss them, seeing if they tasted like I
thought they would
All the while wondering how your kiss would feel if you
trace every inch of my body without stopping
While I use the little bit of breath that I have to whisper your
name repeatedly
I can feel the grip of your hands holding my body not
wanting to let me go
As you whisper my name in my ear and saying that you love
me and any other sweet word
I let my hands travel the nape of your neck and the surface
of your strong broad shoulders
As I can feel your goosebumps starting to form
How I even crave you holding me so close as we sleep
together through the night

As we sleep, I lay my head on your chest to hear that sweet heartbeat of yours
How rapidly it beats the more I listen to it
How can feelings like these have an extremely strong power
How can I not let the feelings inside of me flourish like they should
How can I not describe these indescribable feelings inside of me
How can one person cause me to have so much emotion to the point that they're all that I think about
Please just give me the answers
I just don't want these feelings to ever rest

Tarnished Trust

My trust for you was on lockdown
Me loving you was nothing short of a dream
I strongly considered you as my soul mate
The one who I called my future husband and father to my
children
I thought that my trust for you will never be broken
But it turns out I was wrong
When I found out about your true intentions
All of my trust for you quickly went out the window
The thought of the rest of our lives was no longer there
You broken the trust that I once had for you
While you were the one who seems like you could do no
wrong and was sleeping at night
I was the one who was up at night with a severe amount of
trust issues
Thanks to you, I can't trust anyone else with my love

Dark Love

Some say that certain love is meant to be kept in the dark
Then why are you preventing our love from being shown in
the light
Why are you telling everyone that we're friends in public
But instead we're nothing but lovers in private
Why is it that everytime I come around you in public
I'm nothing more to you than another random girl from the
streets
But in private, you worship me and my body like it's your
temple
Why are you so embarrassed to even be seen with me in
public
But not embarrassed enough to rub up and down my body
the way that you do
But not embarrassed enough to crave some of that God-
forsaken good loving I never fail to give you
Are you the type of person who's ashamed of my public
presence
But often says otherwise when it comes to our private,
promiscuous visits
How you call out my name more times than any given day
So while I was craving the love from you that I have so long
desired
You just simply craved the most simple of satisfaction and
lust
Am I even worth your affection?
Because the worth I may seem to have to you is sexual
attraction

Bad People

I always knew that there were bad people in the world
But the last person I thought it would be is you
Before our love journey took off
You were charming and oh so sweet
You managed to tell me every word I wanted to hear
Sadly I believed and wished I didn't
Your sweet words left without a trace
Replacing them with words that broke my soul
You took me from feeling unstoppable to destructible
You were nothing more than a wolf in sheep's clothing
Now I knew that there were bad people in the world
I just wished you weren't one of them

(The Giver) But Never The Receiver

You have remembered your own heart
But you forgot that I had one of my own
I bent over backwards as you expected me to be in your
corner
But how come you were never in mine to begin with
I have managed to put you on front and center every time
But you kept me in my same rear spot for God knows how
long
I treated you like a high and mighty king
All the while you treated me nothing more than a fool
I have went out of my way for you constantly
But for some reason you wouldn't do the same for me
No matter what I may do for you
You never seem to do the same for me
Was I even your friend to begin with
Or am I nothing more to you than an embarrassment

Cool Summer Dreams

I am laying in my bed on a cool summer night daydreaming. I feel the cool breeze traveling through my window. I daydream about my favorite dream: you. I see and feel your eyes and smile. I can hear your laughter and it's one of my favorite sounds to hear. I feel your arms wrap around my body, keeping me from hurt and pain. Your soft breath is giving me goosebumps on the nape of my neck. As I put my ear against your chest, I timidly hear and feel your heartbeat with my hand and ear. I woke up and felt the other empty cold side of my bed. I cry myself to sleep knowing that my dream will never come true.

Summer of Lies

I met you on a very warm summer day
With mountains of purple and trees of green
I have fell in love with you and your ways
Your heart and personality was keen

I thought you were different in my own eyes
I remember those lively summer nights
Didn't know you were a cheater in disguise
Although I loved with all of my might

One day our relationship took a turn
As you were in the arms of a new love
You left a hole in my heart to burn
I thought I was the only one you dreamt of

Now I wonder what if we did not meet
Now I know that you are full of deceit

Return Home, My Love

I am an elderly woman of 85 years. I hold a book of letters that my beloved has sent to me during our time apart as he went to war. As I sit there and read through each and every letter he has sent me, I transport myself to the time of the war in my younger years. Ever since the end of the war, I took out a small portion of my day to sit on that same old wooden bench outside my front door, waiting for my lover to return like he promised me at the end of each and every letter that he sent me. It seems as though it was yesterday that we embraced and kissed for the very last time before he left to serve the country that he adores. I keep a small picture of him in uniform as it's the only other thing I have of him. Sure, you may think I'm just an 85-year-old woman who's in such severe denial. But what can I really tell you? If you really love that person, they're worth waiting for.

Don't Want To Be The Victim

I want to leap but I'm scared I'll fall
Fall into the arms of the one who ripped my heart to shreds
The one who had no intentions on loving me to begin with
But had every intention on hurting me instead
You said that this time would be different
That you would love me for the better
And not end up hurting me for the worse
How can I even still trust you from what happened the last time
I don't want to jump now and have to face the repercussion later
Don't you remember that actions speak volume
Since the last time you only used your words instead of your actions
So excuse me for not wanting to fall for you so quickly
I just don't want to be the victim of another heartbreak that you caused

Tranquility

When I'm with you, I feel like I'm falling in love for the very
1st time
The amount of serenity I felt around you is unmatched for
How your big, beautiful chestnut eyes sparkle when you talk
about your passions
As well as your face lighting up with pride
How your entire body is overwhelmed with excitement
when we're together
When we're not in each other's beautiful presence
There's not doubt that I'm thinking about you and you only
And I hope that you're thinking about me too
Who knew that serenity can be this beautiful when you're
around me
I never knew that this level of tranquility existed until you
came along
And I sure do hope that you never leave my side

A Message for Her

To the next girl that comes after me
Please I come in peace and not to start drama
I just have a few words for you to know
Now that you're dating the boy that I have once called my own
One: Please treat him the same way I wanted to
With the same love, value, cherishing, and respect that I wanted to give him
Maybe even more than I could've given him
Two: Please be very patient with him
I know it can be very hard at times to be patient with him
Please don't lose your cool the same way I did
Instead, just talk to him about your irritation
Three: Please let your intentions be pure
Although me and him aren't together anymore
He doesn't deserve a single ounce of hurt in the world
Please protect his heart at absolutely all costs
While he's protecting yours as well
Be with him because you actually love him
And not because you show pity on him
The reason why I'm telling you all this is because I never gotten the chance to
I loved him with all my heart but apparently it wasn't enough
So now that you know what you know, please take this with you
You'll need it a hell of a lot more than I do